STRING

INSTRUMENTS

by
John Wood

BEARPORT
PUBLISHING

Minneapolis, Minnesota

Credits

All images are courtesy of Shutterstock.com, unless otherwise specified. With thanks to Getty Images, Thinkstock Photo, and iStockphoto. Recurring – paw, Visual Unit, Trikona. Cover – StockSmartStart, Stave. Page 2–3 – stockphoto-graf. Page 4–5 – AngelaGrant, Pressmaster. Page 6–7 – Joe Bielawa from MInneapolis, USA, CC BY 2.0 <https://creativecommons.org/licenses/by/2.0>, via Wikimedia Commons, aleksandr shepitko. Page 8–9 – Ansis Klucis, trekandshoot. Page 10–11 – Venus Angel, julianne.hide. Page 12–13 – Smerdis, CC BY-SA 4.0 <https://creativecommons.org/licenses/by-sa/4.0>, via Wikimedia Commons, RemarkEliza, rosarioscalia. Page 14–15 – Mindscape studio, TILT Photography. Page 16–17 – Tarisio Auctions.Violachick68 at English Wikipedia, CC BY-SA 3.0 <https://creativecommons.org/licenses/by-sa/3.0>, via Wikimedia Commons, Boiko Y. Page 18–19 – Trofimov Denis, Boris Bulychev. Page 20–21 – Osama Shukir Muhammed Amin FRCP(Glasg), CC BY-SA 4.0 <https://creativecommons.org/licenses/by-sa/4.0>, via Wikimedia Commons, Paolo Terzi, CC BY-SA 3.0 <https://creativecommons.org/licenses/by-sa/3.0>, via Wikimedia Commons, Thesamphotography, mountainpix. Page 22–23 – Martin Good, Jose Retamal, Viktor Cvetkovic, Best smile studio.

Bearport Publishing Company Product Development Team

President: Jen Jenson; Director of Product Development: Spencer Brinker; Managing Editor: Allison Juda; Associate Editor: Naomi Reich; Associate Editor: Tiana Tran; Art Director: Colin O'Dea; Designer: Kim Jones; Designer: Kayla Eggert; Product Development Assistant: Owen Hamlin

Library of Congress Cataloging-in-Publication Data

Names: Wood, John, 1990- author.
Title: String instruments / by John Wood.
Description: Fusion books. | Minneapolis : Bearport Publishing Company,
  2024. | Series: All about instruments | Includes index.
Identifiers: LCCN 2024007025 (print) | LCCN 2024007026 (ebook) | ISBN
  9798889169680 (library binding) | ISBN 9798892324786 (paperback) | ISBN
  9798892321143 (ebook)
Subjects: LCSH: Stringed instruments--Juvenile literature.
Classification: LCC ML750 .W66 2024 (print) | LCC ML750 (ebook) | DDC
  787/.19--dc23/eng/20240213
LC record available at https://lccn.loc.gov/2024007025
LC ebook record available at https://lccn.loc.gov/2024007026

For more information, write to Bearport Publishing, 5357 Penn Avenue South, Minneapolis, MN 55419.

CONTENTS

JOIN THE BAND

Do you love music? Have you ever wanted to play an instrument? Let's join a band!

This book is about string instruments. They use strings to make sound. There are many different kinds of string instruments. Some have been around for thousands of years.

Musicians in a band often play different instruments.

INSTRUMENTS FROM HISTORY

People played bone flutes tens of thousands of years ago.

ABOUT 4,500 YEARS AGO

40,000 YEARS AGO

The Lyres of Ur are some of the oldest string instruments ever found. Some were beautifully decorated.

The djembe drum has been played at many different events for hundreds of years.

ABOUT 800 YEARS AGO

ABOUT 300 YEARS AGO

The serpent was a popular instrument in the 1700s.

7

MAKING SOUND WITH STRINGS

String instruments can be played in different ways. Some musicians pluck the strings with their fingers. Others slide a bow across them. This makes the strings shake, which **vibrates** the air around the them.

You hear the vibrations from string instruments as sounds.

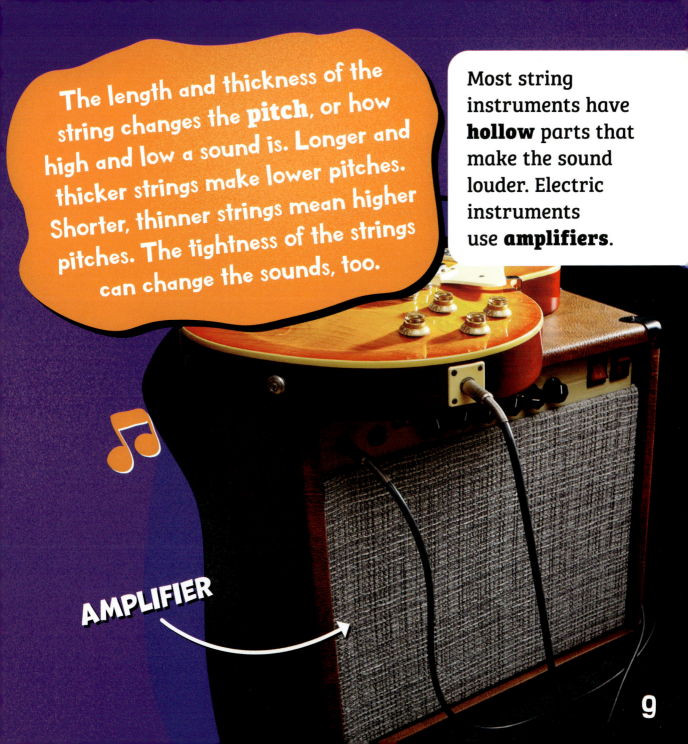

The length and thickness of the string changes the **pitch**, or how high and low a sound is. Longer and thicker strings make lower pitches. Shorter, thinner strings mean higher pitches. The tightness of the strings can change the sounds, too.

Most string instruments have **hollow** parts that make the sound louder. Electric instruments use **amplifiers**.

AMPLIFIER

UKULELE

TUNING PEGS

STRING

BODY

A ukulele is a small instrument with four strings. You **strum** these to make a sound. Ukuleles make quiet, soft sounds with a high pitch.

Ukuleles and most other string instruments have pegs to **tune** the strings.

JAKE SHIMABUKURO

Millions of people have seen videos online of Jake playing the ukulele.

Jake Shimabukuro started playing the ukulele when he was four years old. Today, he is one of the best players in the world.

BASS GUITAR

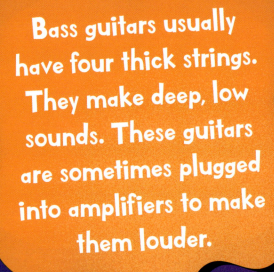

Bass guitars usually have four thick strings. They make deep, low sounds. These guitars are sometimes plugged into amplifiers to make them louder.

AMPLIFIER

BODY

Bass strings are made of metal. Beginner players often get sore fingers from plucking the strings.

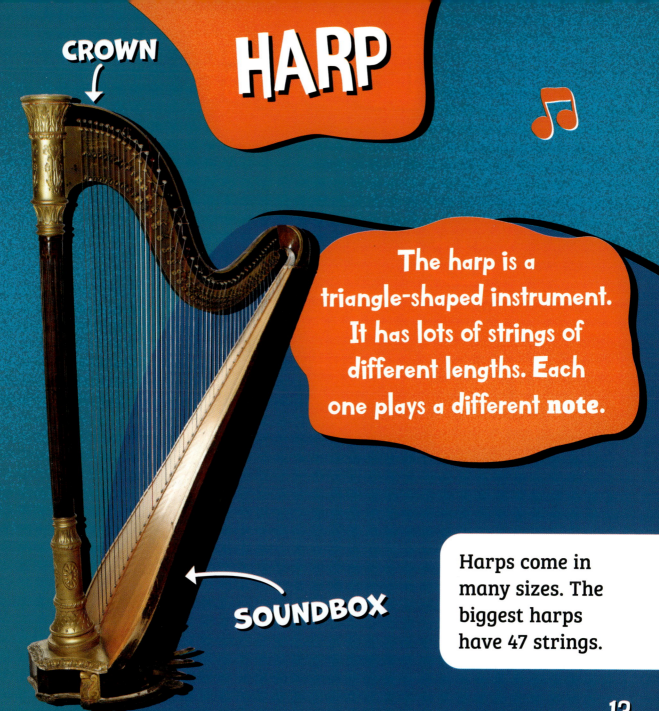

CROWN

HARP

The harp is a triangle-shaped instrument. It has lots of strings of different lengths. **Each** one plays a different **note.**

SOUNDBOX

Harps come in many sizes. The biggest harps have 47 strings.

DOUBLE BASS

TUNING KEYS

The double bass is one of the biggest string instruments. It is taller than most adults! It usually has four thick strings that make very low-pitched sounds.

BOW

Many musicians play the double bass with bows. Bows are made of many long, tightly stretched hairs.

KOTO

TSUME

HEAD

The koto is a popular instrument in **traditional** Japanese music.

Most kotos have 13 strings. These instruments are placed on the floor or on stands when played. Musicians pluck the strings using tsume (soo-MAY), which are small claws worn on their fingers.

GUITAR

ACOUSTIC GUITAR

ELECTRIC GUITAR

Most guitars have six strings that can be plucked or strummed. Acoustic guitars have hollow bodies made of wood. Electric guitars are plugged into amplifiers, which makes them louder and changes the tone of their sound.

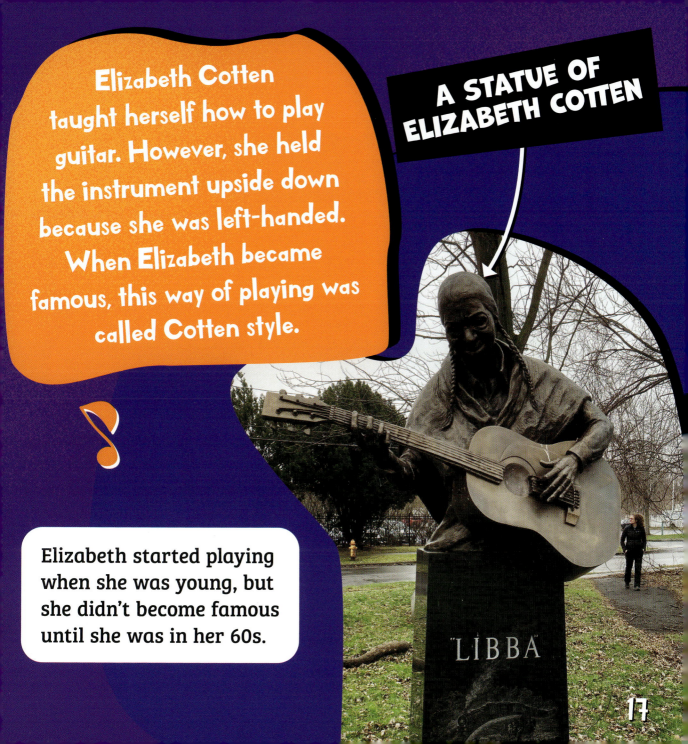

Elizabeth Cotten taught herself how to play guitar. However, she held the instrument upside down because she was left-handed. When Elizabeth became famous, this way of playing was called Cotten style.

A STATUE OF ELIZABETH COTTEN

Elizabeth started playing when she was young, but she didn't become famous until she was in her 60s.

CELLO

PEG

At about 4 feet (1 m) tall, the cello is the second-tallest string instrument. It has four strings that are often played with a bow to make long, smooth sounds.

BOW

ENDPIN

Cellos have endpins that rest on the floor when they are being played.

18

SITAR

TUNING PEG

Most sitars (sih-**TAARZ**) have 18 to 20 metal strings, but a musician plucks only some of them. The other strings shake and make sounds because of the vibrations from the plucked strings.

STRING

BODY

VIOLIN

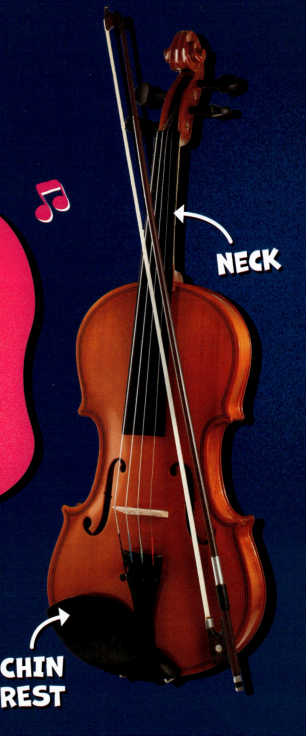

A violin can make very high-pitched notes. It has four strings that are usually played with a bow. The musician tucks the violin under their chin when playing it.

NECK

CHIN REST

Violins are also called fiddles when they play certain kinds of music.

ANTONIO STRADIVARI

Antonio Stradivari was a master violin maker who was born in 1644. Today, the violins he made are so famous that they are worth a lot of money. One violin called the Lady Blunt sold for almost $16 million!

The Lady Blunt

WHAT WILL YOU PLAY?

Now you know all about string instruments! Pick your instrument and join a band.

Violins are often played very fast in Irish folk music.

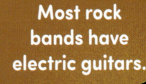

Most rock bands have electric guitars.

The bass guitar is played in many types of music, including blues and pop music.

The harp is usually part of an **orchestra** that plays classical music.

It is time to start playing!

GLOSSARY

amplifiers machines that make sounds louder

hollow empty inside

musicians people who make or play music

note a musical sound of a certain pitch that lasts for a length of time

orchestra a group of musicians who play classical music together

pitch the highness or lowness of a sound

strum to play an instrument by sweeping your fingers across the strings

traditional something that has stayed the same for many years

tune to adjust the musical pitch

vibrates moves back and forth very quickly

INDEX